Ghost to Coast

A Handbook of Ghost
Tours, Paranormal
Investigation Teams, and
Haunted Hotels
Across the Country

By Rhetta Akamatsu

Dedicated to Patrick and Pamela Burns, the Ghost Hounds, Dianna Avena of the Roswell Ghost tour, and all paranormal investigation groups seeking the truth everywhere.

Contents:

My Life, with Ghosts: An Introduction

I am fascinated with the paranormal and paranormal investigation. I'm not completely sure what causes ghostly phenomena, but something does, and I want to know what it is. I've had my own experiences, and I've decided to share them here.

To begin with, my parents practiced an odd sort of belief/disbelief system when it came to ghosts. As staunch Southern Baptists, they didn't believe in them, of course. On the other hand, we had one. It wasn't really a ghost person. It was a ghost car. I used to wonder about that, because obviously cars don't have souls, right? But now I am a very firm believer in residual energy, which I see as being a sort of hologram or audio recording stamped on the air by some event at some point in time, and replaying in an endless loop indefinitely.

As a kid, though, all I knew was that we lived at the end of a dirt road about half a mile from the main road and we were the only house on the road. We had a circular driveway, and every day in the afternoon, around 3 pm, we would clearly hear a car go all away around the house and back out the road. Yet there was no car there. If I was outside playing, I would hear it but never see anything at all. My parents just calmly explained,"Oh, that's the ghost," and let it go at that. They never tried to justify using something they didn't believe in to explain something they didn't understand. They just accepted it. That's odd, I know, but Southerners know that sometimes not believing in something won't keep it from happening.

I was never afraid or worried about the ghost car, and I wasn't worried about the more active spirit that followed me to college at 18, either. I never saw or heard that entity, but it certainly made its presence known. I lived in a dorm room that I shared with a roommate. We shared a bathroom with the next room over. Many times, when my roommate was out and I was studying in the room alone, I would walk into the bathroom, walk back out, and my books would have moved to the floor or the bed. This happened many times. In theory, someone could have opened the door, moved the books, left the room and closed the door, I suppose, but they would have had to be very fast and very silent. Several times, I found the books under my bed. Once or twice, they showed up under there when both my roommate and I were in the room and had been sleeping. But I could justify those times, if I assumed that my roommate was playing a very out-of-character joke on me. But. . .

One weekend my roommate had gone home for the weekend, and so had our suitemates. In fact, that particular weekend only a few people remained in the dorm. I was studying for a test, and I locked the door so I would not be disturbed. I was getting tired, so I decided to take a shower to wake myself up, so I double-checked that the door was locked, as women are prone to do when they are taking a shower in a nearly-empty building. Then I went into the bathroom, turned on the shower, and climbed in. At that time, people still got their music on vinyl, and albums were pretty cheap. I loved music, and I had around 100 albums in the room. I had just got a new Bob Dylan album that week, and it and about 30 other albums were stacked on the floor next to my bed. Yet, when I got out of the shower after about 15 minutes and went back in the room, the albums were nowhere to be found. I was panicking. I checked the door; it was still locked. I checked the one small window; it was secure and someone would have had to climb up two stories to get in it anyway.

I was frantic. I unlocked the door, stepped outside, and there were my albums, all neatly stacked in the hallway right outside the door. I went ballistic. I was so mad I was yelling at the spirit in my room, "Are you crazy? My albums could have been stolen out there! My new Dylan! Leave my stuff alone!"

I must have made an impression, because after that all the pranks stopped. Books quit moving, records stayed put.

I didn't have another experience until years later, after my parents died in the 80's and my first husband and I and our two kids moved into the house I grew up in. Almost immediately, we started waking up at night to the sound of the water running and dishes rattling in the kitchen. It sounded as though someone were washing dishes, but when we checked, of course, no one was in there. Still, in the morning from time to time a few dishes I had left in the sink would be washed, and as the mother of two small children, I was fine with that. A dish-washing ghost was very helpful. I kind of figured it was probably my grandmother, who was a much better housekeeper than I am.

One night, I suppose my slovenly ways may have been a little too frustrating. My husband and I slept next to the kitchen, and we woke up because we heard a strange swooshing noise, followed by a soft thud. I was worried about the kids, but when I checked on them, they were both in their beds, asleep. So my husband and I walked into the kitchen, and there, sticking in the wall behind the kitchen table, was a small butcher knife. The knife was stuck in the wall at about head-height. Even though the doors were locked and no one could have gotten in without our hearing them, we checked the entire house and around the outside, but no one was anywhere around.

I never figured that the ghost who threw it meant to hurt anybody, since the kitchen was empty. I think she was just making a statement about people not washing up at night. It never happened again, but the slit in the wall stayed there for years until we sold the house and the new owner renovated the kitchen.

Since then, I've not had any major experiences with spirits or poltergeists. Another relative had the ghost of a little boy in her house, apparently, and he whispered to me once or twice, "hi!hi!hi!," but as soon as I said hi back, he hushed.

I am very sensitive to the feeling of places, though, and often know facts about houses or locations that I've never read about or visited; not great details but whether there were children there, or if there's a graveyard nearby, or things of that nature.

Oh, there was one other sort of incident related to that. My cousin used to live in a very small trailor. He was divorced and lived alone. He was not a particularly good person, and he did not have a terribly happy life.He died as the result of injuries he received during a robbery and assault that happened when he was away from home, fishing. After he died, my uncle and his wife separated, and my uncle moved into the little trailer briefly, but then he died of a heart attack at age 59, also away from home. I thought that my cousin might have had some things that belonged to my mother, so a few months after my uncle died, two other cousins, my husband, and I went to the little house to see. As soon as we opened the door, the most horrible feeling came over me. I was not really surprised, because I knew that both my cousin and my uncle had suffered from some very mixed-up feelings while living there and, like I said, I'm sensitive to those things. But I had to get out, and I realized if anything of my mother's was in there, I didn't want it. My cousins were anxious to leave, too, although none of us mentioned the feeling, and my husband stayed outside the whole time. This is my second husband, who never lived in the house or knew my cousin, although he had met my uncle briefly. He is not usually sensitive to places at all. But he said to me, "That house had the worse feeling to it that I have ever felt." As far as I know, nobody has gone in there since. I don't think it's haunted, but I do think it soaked up some truly negative energy, and that energy didn't leave when the people did.

So that's my story. All of it's true, and you may choose to believe it or not.

But, like I said, Southerners know that sometimes not believing in things doesn't mean they don't exist.

So, out of this fascination with the paranormal and desire to understand things that are hard to explain, I started Ghost to Coast.us. And from Ghost to Coast.us grew this book. I hope you enjoy reading and using it as much as I have enjoyed putting it together.

Rhetta Akamatsu, May 2007

1. Ghost Tours

NOTE: Tours and websites come and go; these listings were accurate when I published this directory.

The most beautiful and most profound emotion we can experience is the sensation of the mystical. It is the power of all true science. He to whom this emotion is a stranger, who can no longer wonder and stand rapt in awe, is as good as dead. To know that what is impenetrable to us really exists, manifesting itself as the highest wisdom and the most radiant beauty which our dull faculties can comprehend only in their primitive forms-this knowledge, this feeling is at the center of true religiousness. - ALBERT EINSTEIN-

Alabama

Selma, Alabama Ghost Tour

http://www.selmaalabama.com/

Free; available online or get a printed copy at the Visitor's Center

Alaska

Ghosts and Good Time Girls- A Walking Tour of Historic Skagway

http://www.hollandamerica.com/dest/excursion.do?portCode=SGY&tourId=69&dest=A

DURATION: Approximately 2 hours
PRICE: $35 per person

Contact form on website

Arizona

Lost Souls Paranormal Investigations
Tucson Ghost Tours

http://www.assconline.com/ghosttours
.html

$12 per person

LSPI@lostsoulspi.com or call 1-888-
309-5630

Saloon Row Ghost Tour, Williams, AZ

http://saloonrowghosttour.com/

NAU Student Prices :: $10.00 Must
show ID! Regular prices: 15.00 Per
Adult, 8.00 per child(2-12 ages) At
the end of the tour you will receive
your own keepsake certified ghost
hunter card.
Call 928-600-3024

Arkansas

The Eureka Springs Ghost Tours

http://www.eureka-springs-ghost.com/

P.O. Box 189
Eureka Springs, AR 72632
(479)253-6800

California

Haunted Haight Tour

http://www.hauntedhaight.com/html/hauntedhaight_tour.html

$20 per person

1-800-838-3006

San Francisco Ghost Hunt

http://www.sfghosthunt.com/

Prerecorded message: 415-922-5590

The cost is $20 per person, children under 16 $10 and the Ghost Hunt not recommended for kids under 8

The Vampire Tour of San Francisco

http://www.sfvampiretour.com/

Not a ghost tour, but it just sounds like fun

The cost is $20.00 per mortal, or $15.00 each for seniors, students, or groups of 10 or more. The toll free number is 866-4-BITTEN (866-424-8836

Colorado

Colorado Haunted History

http://www.coloradohauntedhistory.com/tours.htm

Adults - $15.00
Children 12 and under - $10.00
Discounts are available for groups over 10 people.

1-888-649-3849 and then press **1**
tours@coloradohauntedhistory.com

Cripple Creek Ghost Walk Tours

http://www.cripple-creek.co.us/ghost.html

PRICE $10 per person
Children under 12 are $5 each and
must be accompanied by an adult.

1-719-689-9113

Gunslingers, Gold, and Ghosts;
Morrison Ghost Walk; Golden Haunted
History

http://atlas.csd.net/~deebeaux/tours.html

Adults $10, 12 and under $5. Private
groups and special tours can be
arranged.
Email: paranormal@csd.net
303-860-8687

Blue Moon Haunted History Tours

http://www.manitoulegends.com/

Hounds from Hell tour $10;
Ghostbusters Tour $20

(719) 685-2409

Connecticut

Haunted Connecticut Tours

http://www.connectionsgrouptours.co
m/signature.html

ConneCTions
PO Box 986, Darien, CT 06820

incoming@connectionsgrouptours.com
fax 203-656-0882;call 203-656-0207
or toll free (US) 866-656-0207

Delaware

Delaware Ghost Tours

http://www.freewebs.com/dgtinc/

Call for price information

For tour dates and times contact us by
phone at (302)365-6282 or email us
at
Delawareghosttours@comcast.net

Florida

Ghost Tours of St. Augustine

http://www.aghostlyexperience.com/

Walking, riding and sailing tours ;
prices from $12 to $15

Phone:(888) 461-1009

Fax: (904)829-1102

P.O. Box 528

St. Augustine, FL 32085

Haunts of The World's Most Famous
Beach (Daytona Beach)

http://www.hauntsofdaytona.com/

This tour is owned by trained, certified
paranormal researcher Doris "Dusty"
Smith of the Daytona Beach
Paranormal Research Society. I have
not had a chance to take the tour yet,
but after meeting and listening to
Dusty at Ghostock 4, I know it would
be a fascinating experience.

HauntsOfDaytona@aol.com

(386) 253-6034.

Tickets are $8 and children under 6
are always free.

Tampa Bay Ghost Tours

http://www.hubbardsmarina.com/ghos
t.html

727.398.5200

Ghost Tours of Amelia Island

http://www.ghosttoursofameliaisland.c
om/tourinfo.html

Fernandina Beach, Florida
904-548-0996
1-866-ghosts0
(1-866-446-7870)

Adults 12 years old and up $15.00
Children 6 years old-11years old $5.00

SPIRITeam

http://spiriteam.org/

Contact form on site

Georgia

Roswell Ghost Tours

http://www.roswellghosttour.com/

TOUR REVIEW:

Roswell is a historic small town in the metro Atlanta area here in Georgia. On Saturday night, September 23, 2006, my husband and I finally took the Roswell ghost tour. The town is near our hometown, so I don't know why we took so long. This is a fascinating two-hour tour and I can't wait to take it again soon.

The only quibble I had with the tour is that since many of the houses are private residences or businesses, and others are in dense residential areas, we were not able to get close at all to them. For instance, at Mimosa Hall, which has a chilling tale attached to it, we had to stand at the end of the driveway and could really not see the house at all. The same was true of

Barrington Hall, considered to be the finest example of Greek Revival architecture in America. We had to stand a block away. I do intend to go back and see them in the daytime, when they are open for tours.

On the other hand, we were able to go right into Founders' Cemetery, and that was my favorite stop on the tour. Our guide, David, was telling us that most "sensitives" are drawn to an area behind founder John Dunwody's grave. I, however, had been to that cemetery once before, and I headed straight to the obelisk-style tombstone of Roswell King, for whom Roswell is named. I put my hand on the tombstone and said something dumb like, "Remember me, buddy?" and my husband snapped a picture. Sure enough, it was the only picture we took in the cemetery that was just full of orbs. In general, I am not that impressed with orbs, but I was very amused that even the pictures we took all around that stone had no strange lights at all.

David told us accounts of hauntings caused by the typical tragic deaths and by events of the Civil War. In our group, there were a number of Roswell natives, and they added their own experiences and stories they had heard, which increased our enjoyment considerably.

We went back to the Roswell tour on Halloween night, when Dianna, the usual host was there. She had Patrick Burns, the creator of Ghost Hounds Paranormal Investigations and co-star of Court TV's Haunting Evidence, as a special guest. They were so friendly and accessible, and aside from the usual tour, we visited one place Dianna usually leaves off, because she thinks it is just too creepy, and so do I. Despite getting a bit freaked out by the "creepy house," I am now willing to say that this is the best ghost tour I've ever taken.

Go, take this tour! I advise taking a flashlight. The brick sidewalks of Roswell are very uneven and in places it is quite dark. I stumbled several times, since my night vision is basically non-existent.

Tour fee is $15 for adults, $10 for children (12 and under) and does not include gratuities for your guide.

770-649-9922

Savannah Ghosts and Gravestones

http://www.trustedtours.com/store/category2.aspx?SID=5&Category_ID=202

$22.50 per adult, $9.00 for children

Reservations are required at least 24 hours in advance as space is limited for this popular tour. Call 912-233-0083

Ghosts and Legends Tour of Savannah

http://www.theghostsofsavannah.com/

Adult: $18.00 ~ Child (8-14): $10.00

Call 866-264-8160

Savannah is a wonderful walking town. It's also a town full of history, and, allegedly, spirits. This is one of the most dramatic tours we ever took. Orphanage fires, duels, hangings, madmen on the loose.. Savannah has had them all.

The walk is easy and covers about a mile altogether. Our guide was knowledgeable and entertaining. No other place I've ever been has such a feeling of history as Savannah. And only Charleston, so far, as seemed so at home with its ghosts.

You will enjoy this walk, and you will not forget it, even if you don't actually encounter any apparitions yourself.

Ghost Talk, Ghost Walk Savannah

http://www.access-savannah.com/ghosttalk.htm

$10 for adults, $5 children 12 and under

912-233-3896 or 1-800-563-3896

Savannah Candlelight Tours

http://ghostsavannah.com/

Email: admin@ghostsavannah.com
Telephone: (912) 6043007
Address: 512 E.Oglethorpe Ave,
Savannah, Ga 31401.

We met this tour owner, James
Caskey, at Ghostock 4 in February
1977. Unfortunately, due to weather
we did not get to take the tour, but we
hope to very soon. Mr. Caskey has a
very interesting official guidebook,
highly recommended whether you take
the tour or not: <u>Haunted Savannah</u>

Ghost Walks-St. Simons Island

http://www.ghostwalkofstsimons.com/

When we took this tour, the official
tour guide was not available and we
were not very impressed with the
guide we had, but the tour itself was
very interesting and the walk was
beautiful. We learned some interesting
things about pirates and some good
ghost stories. There were some highly
unusual noises which the guide told
the kids who were present were cats. I
don't think so! My only complaints
were that our guide really was not

very friendly, and there were very young kids present. The mother of one of the kids kept telling her son that there's no such thing as ghosts really the whole time. What's the point of taking him on a ghost walk, then? But I would definitely say take this tour, if the official guide is available.

Adults $12 / Children (4-12) $6

Call 912-638-2756 or Email: tourgal@bellsouth.net

About Savannah: Savannah is considered one of the most haunted cities in the world, and it has many, many ghost tours. The ones I have included are representative.

Hawaii

Hawaii Chicken Skin Tours

http://www.chicken-skin-ghost-tours-hawaii.hawaiifanatic.com/

Call for tour info

808.943.0371

2634 South King Street, Ste. 3

Honolulu, Hawaii 96826

Idaho

So far, I've found no ghost tours for Idaho.

Illinois

<u>Alton Hauntings Ghost Tours</u>

http://www.altonhauntings.com/

Price range from $20 - $30

Call toll-free at 1-888-446-7859 for Tour Reservations

<u>Chicago Hauntings Ghost Tours</u>

http://www.chicagohauntings.com/

$28 per person; $22 children 8-12

1-888-GHOST-91

ursulabielski@sbcglobal.net

<u>Springfield Hauntings Ghost Tours</u>

http://www.springfieldhauntings.com/

$20 per person

1-888-446-7859

Chicago Supernatural Tours

http://www.ghosttours.com/

PO Box 557544

Chicago, Illinois   60655-7544.

708-499-0300 for further information

Haunted Chicago Land Tours

http://www.ghostresearch.org/tours/

See website for contact info.

Indiana

Haunted Indiana Ghost Walks and Tours

http://www.unseenpress.com/

Walking tours are $15 per person. Seniors (aged 55+) are $10.

Children under 11 are $10. Children under 3 are free. Recommended for children 6 and up.

Reservations can be done online, via email or by calling 317-840-6456.

Iowa

Haunted Iowa City

http://yawp.com/3rd-
i/ADS/ghost/Ghohunt.html

Self-guide, free map online

Haunted Mansion Dinner and Tour

http://www.bigmuddyghosthunters.or
g/id19.html

$49.00 per person, includes a
haunting building history, strange
tales, and eerie stories, plus a
gourmet prime rib dinner, non-
alcoholic beverages, and dessert.

Big Muddy Ghost Hunters
P.O. Box 3002
Dubuque, IA 52004-3002
800-974-7714— additional information
563-542-7487—reservations

Kansas

Wichita Ghost Tours

http://wichitaghosttours.homestead.co
m/downtownghostwalk.html

$8 per ticket

ictghosttours@earthlink.net
or call (316) 807-5615

Kentucky

Ghosts of Old Louisville

http://www.ghostsofoldlouisville.com/thetour.html

Duration: 90 minutes
Cost: $25.00
502-637-2922

Lousiana

Bloody Mary's New Orleans Tours, Events, and Spirit Encounters

http://www.bloodymarystours.com/

". . . a brilliant synthesis of social
history, Mystery and Magic"
— History Channel's Haunted History

Call Bloody Mary's Hotline at (504)
915-7774

fax: (504) 587-0742

The New Orleans Ghost Tour

http://www.neworleansghosttour.com/

Reservations are required and may be made through the web site for the discounted price of $16 for adults, students and seniors.... regular retail prices are $19 for adults, $17 for students and seniors. The $16 price is only offered when making your reservations online with a credit card. Children 12 and under are always free with an adult ticket purchase.

Ghost and Spirit Walking Tour (New Orleans)

http://www.graylineneworleans.com/ghost.shtml

This is a Gray Line Tour

Adult: $22.00
Child: $12.00
Group: $17.75

(504) 569-1401 | (800) 535-7786

Moonlight Mourning

Maine

Ghostly Tours, York

http://www.ghostlytours.com/

Open June 21st to October 30th

$10 per person

Ryan@GhostlyTours.com

1-207-363-0000

Maryland

Fell's Point Ghost Tours

http://www.fellspointghost.com/groups.html

$10/person, groups of 20 or more, or $200 minumum if you have less than 20 people.

Candlelight Ghost Tours of Frederick, Maryland

http://www.marylandghosttours.com/

Adults $8 Children $4

301-668-8922

Ye Haunted History of Olde Ellicott City

http://www.visithowardcounty.com/ghost_tours/index.html

Adults, $6 Kids(12 & under) & Seniors(65+)
Not recommended for kids under 6 years old
Reservations recommended.

Call 1-800-288-TRIP (8747)

ghosts@visithowardcounty.com

Ghosts of Annapolis Tours

http://www.ghostsofannapolis.com/

Zerve at (800) 979-3370 or (212) 209-3370

St. Michaels Ghost Tours

http://www.cruisinthebay.com/ghostto urs.html

$10 per person

Dockside Express Ltd.
P.O. Box 122
Tilghman, Maryland 21671
1-888-312-7847
info@docksidexpress.com

Massachusetts

Ghosts and Gravestones: Boston

http://www.trustedtours.com/store/Gh osts-and-Gravestones-Tour-Boston-C101.aspx

This tours runs on certain dates only. Reservations are required and must be made by calling 617-269-3626. When purchasing eTickets for groups of 20 or more, call Customer Service at 800-213-2474.

$28.80 per adult; $17.10 Children 3-12 (under 3 free)

Vampire and Ghost Tour: Salem

http://www.spellboundtours.com/vampire.htm

$13 Adults, $10 Students/Seniors
$7.00 Children 12 yrs and under
SPELLBOUND TOURS™ (978) 745 –
0138 (in Salem, Massachusetts)

Dead of Night Ghost Tours: Plymouth

http://www.deadofnightghosttours.com/tours.htm

Adults - $13
Children (12 & under) - $10
RESERVATIONS STRONGLY
RECCOMENDED

508 - 866 - 5111 or
508 - 277 - 2371

The Boston Spirits Walking Tour

http://www.newenglandghosttours.com/tours.html

$16 per person; $12 children 8-12

781-235-7149
Email:
jim@newenglandghosttours.com

New England Ghost Tours
P.O. Box 812128
Wellesley, MA 02482-0014

Michigan

Shadows Beyond the Veil

http://profile.myspace.com/index.cfm?fuseaction=user.viewprofile&friendid=176084960

$13.00/ per person. Children 12 & under $8.00

Visit the MySpace page for more information

Minnesota

So far, I have found no ghost tours of Minnesota.

Mississippi

Natchez Ghost Tours

http://www.visitnatchez.com/custom/
webpage3.cfm?content=content&id=8
7

Adults $12 Children 12 and under $7
Tuesday through Saturday, beginning
at 7:30 p.m. Tickets are available at
Fydeaux's Pet Company, 207 State St.
or to reserve tickets call 601-445-
8811

Vicksburg Historical Ghost Tours

http://www.vicksburgcvb.org/tours/in
dex.html

1100 Washington Street
601-636-0611
Adults $6, Children $4
8 pm or 8:30 pm Spring and Fall, Call
for schedule

Columbus Ghost Tour

http://www.columbus-
ms.org/group_travel/full_day.html

To plan your next trip to Columbus,
please contact Mandy Wells, Group

Travel Manager at (800) 327-2686 or email at mandy@columbus-ms.org.

Missouri

Haunted Historic Hannibal, Missouri

http://tours.rockcliffemansion.com/

Tickets: $15 Tour Only $25 Tour/Lunch

Palm Readings are available for an additional $10 fee.

TICKETS AVAILABLE ONLY ONLINE OR BY CALLING 573.221.4140 or 877.423.4140.

St. Louis Spirit Search Tours

http://www.stlspiritsearch.com/

Cost: $15 per person (as of January 1, 2007)
CASH ONLY!
RESERVATIONS ARE ALWAYS REQUIRED
This tour is NOT recommended for anyone under the age of 16
RESERVATIONS MUST BE MADE BY PHONE
Call 314.776.466

Montana

None so far.

Nebraska

None so far; do you know of one?
Contact starmac@comcast.net

Nevada

Haunted Vegas Tours

http://www.hauntedvegastours.com/

$48.25 for tour and show; $59.25 for VIP which includes color photo and set of dowsing rods.

VegasExplorers.com
Greek Isles Casino Box Office
Phone: (702) 737-5540
Greek Isles Casino
305 Convention Center Drive
Las Vegas, Nevada 89109

Reno Mystery History Ghost Walk

http://www.renoghostwalk.com/

Tickets are $20.00 for adult and $10.00 for children 10 and over. Under 10 walks free.

Check or money order to

Tickets@Thunder Mountain
Productions
PO Box 19514
Reno, NV 89511

New Hampshire

New England Curiosites Walking Tours: Portsmouth, NH

http://www.newenglandcuriosities.com

Features a variety of ghost tours; prices vary

New England Curiosities Walking Tours
c/o Roxie Zwicker
PO Box 4263, Portsmouth, NH 03802
phone: 207-439-8905

roxie@newenglandcuriosities.com

New Jersey

Ghost Tour of Ocean City ,NJ

http://www.ghosttour.com/ocean_city.htm

PRICES: $13 per adult ($7 ages 4-12)
OceanCity@ghosttour.com

Phone: 609-814-0199

Rutgers New Brunswick/Piscataway Campus Ghost Tour

http://campusinfo.rutgers.edu/ghosttour

Subject to the availability of the Knight Guide staff, the Ghost Tour of Rutgers may be scheduled year-round for a nominal fee.

723/932-9342 x2619

Haunted Cape May Tour

http://www.hauntednewjersey.com/capemaytour/index.html

See website for information

<u>Elaine's Haunted Mansion Ghost Tour.</u>
<u>Cape May</u>

http://www.elainesdinnertheater.com/
ghost.html

Adults: $10.00
Children: $5.00
Call for more information609-884-
4358

New Mexico

<u>Old Town Ghost Tours</u>

(Albuquerque)

http://www.toursofoldtown.com

GHOST Tours are held NIGHTLY at
8:00pm

Call for more information: (505) 246-
TOUR

$20.00 Adults ; $15.00 Seniors (62 &
up), Active Military, Students (ages
13-17)

$10.00 Youth (ages 6-12)

Children ages 5 and under are FREE
(when accompanied by an adult)

<u>Ghostwalkers </u>(Santa Fe)

http://www.historicwalksofsantafe.co
m/santaFeGhostWalkerTour.htm

Ghostwalkers: $13 / person;
Ghostwalkers Especial: $17.50/person,
10 person minimum, please call ahead
for reservations, 505.986.8388.
Email: historicwalksofsf@earthlink.net

NEW YORK

<u>Ghosts of New York</u>

http://www.ghostsofny.com/

Including tours centered about Edgar
Alan Poe, Ghosts of Greenwich Village,
etc.

$15 per person

P.O. Box 656780 Flushing, NY 11365-
6780
(718) 591-4741
drphil@newyorktalksandwalks.com

<u>The Spooks of New York City</u>

http://www.artsandmusicpa.com/trave
lpanyc/nycghosts.htm

Use this list of sites to create your own
tour.

North Carolina

<u>Beaufort Ghost Walk</u>

http://www.tourbeaufort.com/ghostwa
lk.htm

Adults - $10 -- Kids under 12 - $8

(252) 342-0715

<u>Asheville Haunted Ghost Tours</u>

http://ghostandhaunt.com/tour.php?id
=1

RESERVATIONS REQUIRED
(828) 355-5855

ADULTS $17 CHILDREN $9
8 to 14 years old. 7 and under free.

North Dakota

None so far

Ohio

Haunted Heartland Tours

http://hauntedhistory.net/

There's a lot of information at this website; check it out for tour contacts

Lantern Tour of the Ghosts of Zoar

http://www.haunted-ohio.com/pages/lntrn.htm

Cost is $16.00 per person.

330-874-2002

Haunted Cleveland

http://hauntedcleveland.net/

(216) 251-0406
info@hauntedcleveland.net

Oklahoma

Tulsa Spirit Tours

http://www.pittok.com/events/Ghost%20Tours/ghost_tours.html

Tickets: $30.00 each
PITTfounder@cox.net

P.I.T.T.
P.O. Box 803
Broken Arrow, OK 74013

Tulsa Hex House 1944

<u>Historical Haunting Tours of Oklahoma</u>

http://www.ghouli.com/oklahoma_gho
st_hunting_classes_a.htm

$15 per person

tonya@ghouli.com

Oregon

<u>Haunted Shanghai Tunnel Tours</u>

http://www.ghostsandcritters.com/sha
nghai%20tunnel%20walks.html

See website for tour information

Pennsylvania

Sleepy Hollow of Gettysburg
Candlelight Tours

http://www.sleepyhollowofgettysburg.
com/

Phone: 717-337-9322
Fax: 717-337-9327

 ghostwalks@desupernet.net

$7 per person; $13 for "Catch the
Spirits" tour

Ghost Tour of Philadelphia

http://www.ghosttour.com/Philadelphi
a.htm

From $8 to $15

Signers Garden
5th & Chestnut Streets
Philadelphia, PA 19106
Phone: (215) -41-3-1997
E-Mail: ghosttour@ghosttour.com

Ghost Tour of Lancaster County

http://www.ghosttour.com/lancaster.h
tm

$14 per person; $8 4-12

Email: Lancaster@ghosttour.com
Phone: 717-687-668

Ghosts of Gettysburg Candlelight Tour

http://www.ghostsofgettysburg.com/

271 Baltimore Street
Gettysburg, PA 17325

Phone: (717) 337-0445
reservations@ghostsofgettysburg.com

History and Mystery Tours of Philadelphia

http://members.tripod.com/phillyGhos
ts/index.html

Cost: $20 per person. Children under
12, FREE

P.O. Box 3611

Philadelphia, PA 19125
Tel: 1-877-PA Ghost (1-877-724-
4678)

or: 215-423-3930
Fax: 215-423-3930
E-Mail: - HstryMstry@aol.com

Rhode Island

Ghost Tours of Newport, RI

http://www.ghostsofnewport.com/

Newport, Rhode Island
Phone: 401-841-8600
Toll Free: 1-866-33GHOST

Adults $18; Kids $10

South Carolina

Ghosts and Legends Of Charleston

http://www.charlestonghosts.com/

Feature Review

Stand in a narrow cobblestone alley and listen to the tale of a bloody duel. . . listen for the sound of a whistling doctor.. .learn the legend of the "grey man,". . . maybe encounter a spectre or two yourself. Either way, the Ghosts and Legends tour of Charleston lets you gaze into Charleston's past, and enables you see and feel this fabled city in a way you never could before.

Charleston, like Savannah, seems comfortable with its ghosts. They are an inextricable part of the culture for many. Whether you believe, or whether you don't, the stories for the most part can be confirmed, and there is a communion with the past that stems most directly from standing there, in the very spot.. where a foolishly brave man died, where a broken heart led to a suicide, where a home was so loved the owner vowed she would never leave it.

And, who knows? Opening yourself to a new experience could just lead to a whole new level of your world as you know it.

So come out and see what Charleston's ghosts have in store for you. There are many ghost tours in Charleston; I have only taken this one. I can guarantee that the guides know how to tell a story; that they have their facts straight, and that you will be entertained and enlightened, whether you encounter the spirits with your eyes or with your heart.

Adults: $18.50 Children(8-14): $10.50

Call Toll-Free: 1-866-550-8939

The Ghosts of Carolina Tour-Columbia

http://www.columbiatours.net/tours/to
urDetail.cfm/tid/2448

$15.95 per adult; $3 discoun on the
Internet; $10 child

Beaufort, SC Ghost Tours

http://www.beauforttraveler.com/see_
the_sights/tours/ghost.shtml

Phone: 843-575-4967

Charleston Ghost and Dungeon
Walking Tour

http://www.bulldogtours.com/charlest
on-sc-ghost-tour.html

Cost: Adults -$18 per person;
Children (7-12) - $10.00

We took this tour on May 26, 2007.
Frankly, I was disappointed. The tour
lasts for 90 minutes, but the dungeon
part is only about 10 minutes of that.
The dungeon is very small, and filled
with animatronics and other displays.
While our guide told us some
interesting things about the patriots
and pirates who were imprisoned in
this dungeon in the 1700's, she never
once mentioned ghosts. After we left
the dungeon, our guide, Nancy, took
us on quite a long and silent walk to
the waterfront. Charleston is one of
the most haunted cities in the world,
and yet we made no stops and heard
no stories for at least 20 minutes. At
the waterfront, Nancy told us an
interesting story about a ghost car
that used to haunt the old Cooper
River bridge, and showed some
interesting pictures. We also visited a
fascinating haunted brewery and the
famed Philadelphia alley, which was a
notorious duelling site as well as a site
for illicit encounters of other types.
The ghost story Nancy told there was
a interesting one, too, but that made a
total of 3 ghost stories for a 90 minute
tour. This tour had the least stops and
the least stories of any ghost tour I've
ever been on in fact. I think it is

because Bulldog tours, which runs this one, has several other haunted tours, including Ghosts and Graveyards and the Haunted Jail, and they have just divided their tours up so much that they can not include much in any one, unless the others are more inclusive than this one was. Charleston has a lot of ghost tours; I would pick another one.

http://www.bulldogtours.com/charleston-sc-ghost-tour.html

Cost: Adults -$18 per person
Children (7-12) - $10.00

Bulldog Tours, Inc.
40 North Market St.
Charleston, SC 29401
843-722-8688 – fax

Other ghost tours are also available from Bulldog Tours, including

Ghost and Graveyard Walking Tour-Charleston

Cost: $18 per person

Aiken Ghost Tours

http://www.discoversouthcarolina.com
/products/26167.aspx

Adults $15; age 12 and younger,
seniors and college students $10

144 Jasper St.
Aiken,SC 29801

Phone: (803) 270-3683

About Charleston:

Charleston used to have about 6 ghost
tours. Now it seems to have about 20.
I have not chosen to list all of them,
but rest assured that there are
coupons and brochures all over town
for them.

Myrtle Beach Ghost Walk

http://www.ghostshows.com/ghostwal
k.html

info@ghostshows.com

Barefoot Landing

4818 Hwy.17S.

North Myrtle Beach, South Carolina
29582
Phone: (843) 361-2700

South Dakota

Deadwood Ghost Tours

http://www.ghosttraveller.com/south_
dakota.htm

A build-your-own tour with
descriptions of allegedly haunted
locations

TENNESSEE

Nashville Ghost Tours

http://www.nashvilleghosttours.com/

Starts: 8:00 PM Wednesday-Monday
at: The Hermitage Hotel, 6th Ave. N &
Union Ave

Costs $13 Adults

$8 Children (7-11); Under 6 free

FEATURE REVIEW

Who is buried in the walls of the
Capitol building? What is the ghostly
secret of St. Mary's Cathedral?

Find out the answers to these and
other questions as you follow your
lantern-bearing guide on a 90-minute,
1/2 mi easy trek around downtown
Nashville.

Our tour was the first one of the
season. About eight of us met our
friendly, informative guide in front of
the Hermitage Hotel, home of the
famous "white lady." We were told
that there have been many sightings
of the lady on the tour, but we did not
encounter her personally, nor, indeed
any other of the ghostly apparitions
we learned of. Nevertheless, the tour
was a great way to see some of
Nashville at night and get a taste of
history. From Rachel Jackson and a
couple of other famous ghosts at the

Capitol to Chet Atkins at the Ryman, we covered them all. My favorite was the mysterious and odd story of St. Mary's.

Personally, I would not bring small children on this tour, as it does cover a very adult section of town, Printer's Alley. (I was fascinated to learn here that when you see a building with a balcony in downtown Nashville, it probably used to be a brothel.) The walk is very easy and there are a lot of stops. Wear comfortable shoes, and bring a camera. We haven't looked at all our pictures yet. I hear that often things show up that weren't visible to the eye. Who knows?

Ghost Tours at Carnton

http://www.carnton.org/Ghosttours.htm

Adults $10, Seniors $9, Children 6-12 $5, 5 and under free

615-794-0903

info@carnton.org.

Smoky Mountain Ghost Tours

http://www.hauntingstour.com/smokies/

Adults $15, Scouts and children 6-14 $5, 5 and under free; 865-430-9255

Appalachian Ghost Walks

http://www.appalachianghostwalks.com/

Contact for prices and discount travel packages

P.O. Box 153

Unicoi, TN 37692 USA.

Reservations and Info: (423) 743-WALK (9255)
Email: Info@AppalachianGhostWalks.com

Haunted Ghost Tours-Gatlinburg

http://ghostandhaunt.com/tour.php?id
=4

RESERVATIONS REQUIRED
(865) 366-5834
ADULTS $17 CHILDREN* $9
8 to 14 years old. 7 and under free

Bell Witch Cave-Adams, TN

http://www.prairieghosts.com/b-
cave.html

Not technically a ghost tour, but a
must-see for paranormal enthusiasts

Read the story on the website!

$7 per person

(615) 696-3055

Bell Witch House

Texas

There's supposed to be a ghost with a banjo in this picture. Do you see it?

Haunted Texas Tours

http://www.ghostsoftexas.com/

See website for prices

(512) 853-9826

Ghost Tours of Galveston

http://www.geocities.com/peterh1@pr odigy.net/ghosttoursofgalveston.html

$15 adults; $10 children under 12

281-339-2124 - Tour Office

For Next Tour Time Call GHOSTLINE
409-949-2027

High Spirits Tours-Houston

http://www.highspiritstours.com/

Tours for groups of 20 or more only at present.

See website to email for info

Hauntings History of San Antonio

http://www.webspawner.com/users/g hosttour/

$10 for adults; 7-17 $5; under 7 free

CALL: 210-348-6640

Utah

None so far.

"Any unexplained phenomenon passes through three stages before the reality of it is accepted. During the first stage, it is considered laughable. During the second stage, it is adamantly opposed. Finally, during the third

stage, it is it is accepted as self-evident."
—Arthur Schopenhauer -19th century German philosopher

Vermont

<u>Stowe at Night Lantern Tours</u>

http://www.govtn.com/memberdetails.asp?load=267

$8 adults; $4 students 8-18, children free

Shawn or Mary Woods
118 Stowebury Road
Waterbury Center, VT 05677
(802)244-1173
Newf1Ted@aol.com

Virginia

<u>Leesburg, VA Ghost Tour</u>

http://www.vsra.net/

Adults are $10, kids 12 and under are $5

Small children will not be charged

See website to email for info

Alexandria's Original Ghost and
Graveyard Tour

http://www.alexcolonialtours.com/gra
veyard.html

$10 for guests 18 years old and older.
$5 for guests between the ages of 7
and 17.
Ages 6 and under come for free.
Phone 703-519-1749
Email: tours@alexcolonialtours.com

Haunts of Richmond

http://www.hauntsofrichmond.com/ho
me.htm

To purchase tickets by phone, please
call Zerve at
(800) 979-3370 or (212) 209-3370

Williamsburg Ghost-Lantern Tours

http://www.williamsburgprivatetours.c
om/ghost.htm

Prices vary

WilliamsburgTours@cox.net

Virginia Beach Ghost Tours

http://www.williamsburgprivatetours.com/VA%20Beach%20Ghsot%20Tours.htm

Group tours: $96 for up to 8 people, $12 each additional person; 757 897-9600

Washington (State)

Haunted Happenings: A Seattle Ghost Tour

http://www.privateeyetours.com/haunted.htm

This is a van tour. $25 per person

(206)365-3739

Spooked in Seattle Tours

http://www.spookedinseattle.com/

Email spookedinseattle@aol.com for tour info.

Pike Place Market Ghost Tour-Seattle

http://www.marketghost.com/

$10 per person

206-322-1218

WASHINGTON, DC

Capital Hauntings

http://www.zerve.com/WashWalks/CapHaunt

$10 per person

Tickets through Zerve: visit website to purchase

West Virginia

Haunted Parkersburg Ghost Tours

http://users.wirefire.com/magick/

Adults $8.00, Seniors & Students $7.00;

Children 13 & Under $6.00,6 & Under FREE.

(304) 428-7978; No reservations required!

<u>West Virginia Hauntings Tours and Events</u>

http://www.wvtourism.com/hauntings/calendar.asp

Several tours featured; prices vary

See the website for contacts and more info

<u>West Virginia Penitentiary Ghost Hunts</u>

http://www.wvpentours.com/

Groups of at least 20; $20 per person

818 Jefferson Ave.
Moundsville, WV
304.845.6200

Wisconsin

<u>Burlington Haunted Tours</u>

http://www.burlingtonnews.net/haunt
edtours4.html

$20 per person

262 767 2864

Wyoming

<u>Casper Living History Ghost Tour</u>

http://www.paintedpast.org/WalkingTo
urs.html

For more information contact
Painted Past Enterprises - Donna
Fisher
307-267-7243 fax: 307-472-4331

In My House
By Mitch Dobner

In my house I live as a ghost

I died so many years ago

I haunt the rooms I love the most

Although in daylight I lay low

I want to speak to you direct

As no one seems to hear my words

I'm not quite sure what you expect

When you invade my house in herds

You group together, ask for "signs"

Showing me no signs of leaving

You've no respect for what is mine

Just because you are still breathing

You ask for proof that I am there

But as I can no longer speak

I only throw things in the air

And also make an old door creak

The validation given out

You panic then you run away

Running out of the room you shout

Just when I thought that you would stay

You flee the house into the night

Breathing until the moment's passed

I do not understand your fright

I only did what I was asked

You ask me to communicate

I do the best that I can do

You run outside through my front gate

Then I am just a joke to you

I may not live or breathe the air

I am no longer flesh and bone

But what you're doing is not fair

You leave me in this house alone

I do have feelings that are hurt

When you all curse and run from me

You treat me as though "dead" means "dirt"

I only want you all to see

That I live here without a friend

I would just like some company

For being dead is not the end

Why can't you be a friend to me

I couldn't have said it better myself. Until we know what spirits are, let's assume they have feelings, and treat them with respect.

How To Conduct A Paranormal Investigation
By Rhetta Akamatsu

Paranormal investigations have become very popular these days, mostly due to such popular TV shows as "Ghost Hunters" and "Most Haunted." Ghost hunting can be a fun, educational, exciting, and sometimes scarey, way to explore the past and the present. But, as in any other endeavor, there are right ways and wrong ways to approach the activity.

Let me say right here that I am no expert in the field. "There are no experts in this field," one of the speakers at Ghostock 4 Paranormal Convention said earlier this month, "only people with more experience." I've been reading about, watching, and listening to those people with more experience, and I've picked up some how to hints I'd like to share.

* First, get permission before you explore.

It is unwise, unsafe, and often unlawful to enter abandoned buildings or cemeteries at night. Obviously, it would be rude to enter anyone else's property to "ghost-hunt" without their explicit permission to do so. Ask before you enter!

* Have the right attitude.

It is not necessary to believe in ghosts or spirits to conduct a paranormal investigation properly, but it is necessary to keep an open mind. A certain amount of skepticism is good, and will keep you from interpreting every little creak or speck of dust as paranormal phenomena. However, if you are convinced that nothing is going to happen, your mind will automatically discount anything that does, and you will not experience anything. Acknowledge that unexplained things do happen, but debunk whatever you can.

* Have the right equipment.

There are different schools of thought about this. Some people like to work with psychics and mediums, and trust the judgement of their eyes, ears, and feelings above any other evidence. I think that feelings are very important, and so is personal observation. But these things are not provable or quantifiable. Some equipment that might help catch something closer to evidence would be a tape recorder, for

"EVPs", or Electronic Voice Phenomena, spoken words which do not belong to anyone present on the scene; cameras(both digital and regular film for best results); EMF readers, to measure electromagnetic fields (which some people believe are usually present when there is paranormal activity in an area,) and digital cameras to measure changes in temperature, which also seem to often occur when unusual events take place.

* Do not take chances with things you do not understand.

No matter what you believe, do not taunt or tease or try to anger ghosts or spirits. Be very careful about using ouija boards and other such gadgets to communicate with spirits. It is inexcusably arrogant to assume that we know everything there is to know about negative energy, the afterlife, or any other area outside the norm, which is, after all, what "paranormal" means.

* Don't go alone.

Yes, people have been harmed by poltergeist activity, although that is extremely rare. More commonly, people may be overwhelmed by emotion or fear and might suffer panic attacks or other emotional episodes. Aside from that, many investigation locations may be old or in poor repair and injury or falls can happen. So always have a partner.

* Be patient. Understand that many, many times nothing at all is going to happen for hours, if ever. Paranormal investigations involve sometimes long stretches of doing nothing but sitting quietly and observing. Only embark on this kind of activity if you feel that the possibility of catching something extraordinary is worth a lot of time and effort.

* Study. Read. Watch. Learn. The more you know about paranormal history, other people's experiences, and the latest equipment and techniques, the more rewarding your experience will be.

Remember, you don't have to subscribe to any particular theory to investigate the paranormal; just accepting that we don't know everything and things do happen outside the ordinary that are unexplainable is enough. And wanting to learn more about those things is a legitimate area of study.

Paranormal investigation is a fascinating field, and with the right attitude, can be rewarding on many levels. The key is attitude. Keep your mind open and be prepared for anything or nothing!

Ghost Hunting 101
By Dr. Rita Louise

Do you hear bumps in the night? Does your hair stand on end when you walk into a room? Maybe you feel as if someone is watching you or perhaps you think you see someone out the corner of your eye, but when you turn to look no one is there? What you may be encountering in those unsettling moments is a ghost. So before you go running out of your house screaming, let's take a moment to talk about ghostly encounters and those that investigate this phenomena.

A ghost is believed to be the spirit or soul of a person who has remained on Earth after death. When a ghost has taken up residence in a location, it is referred to as a haunting. There are two different ways in which a ghost inhabits a location. The most common type of haunting is a residual haunting. A residual haunting is typified by ghostly energy that is static or goes through a number of movements over and over again. It can be likened to watching a movie clip that repeats itself or a record album that has a skip in it, causing the needle to jump back to an earlier point on the album and begin again.

The second classification of haunting is the classic haunting. In a classic haunting the ghost displays intelligence and interacts with the people in the environment. It is not uncommon during a classic haunting for items to be moved around, for lights or electrical appliances to turn on and off, to hear voices our sounds out of nowhere or to be touched, tickled, stroked or even shoved. These ghosts often reflect the personality of an individual, even after their death. With this type of haunting, the aroma of flowers, perfume, cigarette smoke or other scents that are associated with the individual are often detected.

So whether you think you are being haunted by a ghost and want to have a group of trained professionals to come to your home or are interested in investigating all that goes bump in the night, but don't know where to begin, here's some information that can help you get started.

It is held that ghosts are electro-magnetic in origin and they create these fields when trying to manifest into this dimension. The energy that is given off by a ghost causes disruptions in the locations magnetic field, thus making it detectable by specialized equipment and psychics alike.

Because the presence of a ghost can be detected by specific types of equipment, a ghost hunter can become well equipped with a number of affordable pieces of equipment, many of which you may already own. From basic to advanced, there are many different types of equipment you can use to detect an otherworldly presence. For someone thinking about participating in an investigation, this doesn't mean you have to own every piece of equipment in order to perform a reliable investigation. It does mean that you should at least possess a basic set of tools to use.

Basic Equipment

35mm or Digital Camera – For a beginner, having a camera is probably the easiest and least expensive way to begin. Pictures, whether digital or recorded on film can capture paranormal activity, activity that is often invisible to the naked eye. This is especially true in the case of documenting the presence of orbs and ectoplasm.

Notebook & Pen or Pencil – Simple as

this may be, it is always a good idea to have something to record any notes, findings or experiences you may have during an investigation.

Flashlight – Many times an investigation will take you to a dark or foreboding location such as a cemetery, old warehouse, abandoned building or other place that is dark or without electricity. In these instances you will need to have a portable light source.

Extra Batteries – Depending on the paranormal activity of a location, batteries oftentimes will mysteriously and unexpectedly lose their charge leaving you in the dark. Regardless of the type of equipment you use, make sure you bring extra batteries along to replenish depleted ones.

Intermediate Equipment

EMF Detector – The Electromagnetic Field Detector is probably one of the most important pieces of equipment to own if you are serious about doing an investigation. In addition to detecting the energy fields of ghosts, it is a key tool to use when taking baseline readings of a site. A baseline reading is a preliminary evaluation of a

85

location, where investigators identify any existing or man made electromagnetic fields such as those created by power lines or electrical appliances.

Digital Video Camera – Video cameras can be a useful investigation tool. Unlike still cameras, a video camera will document any activity in its entirety including the length of time the phenomena occurs, the surrounding conditions, as well as the phenomena itself. A tripod to rest the video camera on is also helpful, especially if it is going to be left in a stationary position to record the activity in a specific location.

Tape Recorder with an External Microphone – There is no better way to capture EVP's (electronic voice phenomena) than through the use of a tape recorder. Whether using a traditional tape recorder with high quality tapes or a digital recorder, an external microphone should always be used. A detached mic will eliminate the sounds of internal gears and turning wheels that can contaminate your recording.

Advanced Equipment

Motion Detectors – Motion detectors
can be used to sense the movement of
unseen forces. Many need to be
plugged in to an outlet, but battery
operated ones are also available.
Before you go out and buy one, decide
which type will best support you
investigatory needs.

Thermal Scanner – A thermal scanner
or non-contact thermometer can be
used to detect rapid temperature
changes. A change of ten degrees or
more from the ambient temperature
(the temperature of the surrounding
area) can indicate an ethereal
presence.

Psychics – As An Investigative Tool

In addition to tools such as cameras,
meters and gauges that are used by
ghost hunters, many groups also
utilize the services of trained psychics
as a means of gathering information
about a site. This is the role I play
when working with ghost hunting
groups.

Finding a true psychic to work with can
be a real asset to the quality of your
investigation. They can play an
invaluable role in supporting the
efforts of any paranormal

investigation. Like a good piece of equipment, a psychic can help to detect anomalies as well as provide additional insights into the nature of activity encountered.

If your group decides to include the use of a psychic as part of the investigation team, there are a few items that should be considered. To maximize the objectivity of the investigation, it is critical that the psychic go into a location "cold". This means that they do not know the details of the location or of any activity that may have been encountered by other members or the property owner. Telling the psychic the history of a property can cause the individual to become "contaminated", which can make it difficult for them to differentiate what they perceive from what they have been told.

Conducting An Investigation

With at least a basic kit of equipment in hand, you are now ready to explore the world of paranormal phenomena. Before you begin, there are a few ground rules to consider. First, never go on an investigation alone, in addition to personal safety, you never know what may happen. Next, consider the fact that ghost hunting groups are often judged by their behavior and professionalism – so always try to be respectful of the people, places and situations you may encounter.

To do an investigation, the first step is to select a location. Locations can include cemeteries, old buildings, historic sites, private homes and businesses. Always get permission to be on a site. This will keep you from getting in trouble for trespassing. Before you begin a formal investigation it is a good idea to do some research on the site. Talk to the owner, check out old newspapers, or contact the local historic society to see if anything happened there in the past. It is also a good idea to evaluate the terrain for potential hazards or/or to identify places where you can setup stationary video cameras, motion detectors or tape recorders.

Most investigations occur after dark, between the hours of 9pm and 6am. These hours are considered the "psychic hours" and are believed to be the best time to record paranormal activity.

When you get to the selected location,

walk around to get a feel for it. Next, set up any stationary equipment and take baseline readings of the site. Then let the investigation begin. Take pictures, shoot video, record for EVP and take meter readings. Take them everywhere and anywhere, especially if you feel something or get a reading on another piece of equipment. When you are done walking around a site, turn your stationary equipment on and let it run while you and your group are out of the area.

When you have finished collecting your data, it is time for analysis. Here each picture, video and tape is reviewed for evidence of a haunting. This is probably the most important part of any investigation. As you review your materials, be skeptical. Look for earthly causes of any phenomena. Was someone smoking in the area? Was the room or location dusty? Where there reflective surfaces that could be the cause of the anomaly in your image? It is important to make sure your evidence will stand up to scrutiny by eliminating any other explanations. This will give your data more credibility.

As you pore over your data, what you will find is that not every location you go to will have ghostly activity. You may discover that many of the things you initially detected during your investigation actually have real world explanations as opposed to supernatural ones. What keeps many ghost hunters going is that one-in-five chance that this investigation will be the "real" thing.

When your analysis is done, presenting your finding to the home or property owner or sharing your results with others is often done. Many groups also post the results of their investigations on their group's website, thus share the outcome of their investigation with the rest of the world.

If you are interested in ghost hunting or think your have a ghost hanging around in your local, there is a plethora of information available on the worldwide web. Here you can find articles about ghost hunting in general, stories of other people's ghostly encounters, places that sell ghost hunting equipment and even sites hosted by ghost hunting groups in your geographic area.

So if you think you are hearing bumps in the night, don't be afraid – it just might be a ghost!

Dr. Rita Louise, Ph D is a Naturopathic
Physician and the founder of the
Institute Of Applied Energetics. It is
her unique gift as a medical intuitive
that enlivens her work. Visit
http://www.soulhealer.com or
http://www.appliedenergeticsinstitute
com for more information.

Alabama

Alabama Foundation for Paranormal Research

http://www.alabamaparanormal.org/

Angieb@AlabamaParanormal.org

O.R.B.S.

http://www.angelfire.com/ab5/orbs/

See website for info

Alabama Ghost Hunting

http://geocities.com/alabamaghosthunting/

See website for info

Alabama Ghost Hunters Society

http://ghostinvestigator.tripod.com/ghostinvestigators/index.html

ghostinvestigator@yahoo.com

Ghost Hunters of the South (Mobile, AL)

http://www.ghots.net/

See website for contact form

North-Eastern Alabama Paranormal Society

nealparasociety@aol.com

Alaska

IOPIA

http://hometown.aol.com/__121b_SFY
2QDQTBcAZkkhofcA3qYxTXXpj/U4YIpA
IPcpIVR+GPfViBGLHmQ

Visit website for info

Arizona

Arizona Paranormal Investigations

http://www.arizonaparanormalinvestigations.com/

info@arizonaparanormalinvestigations.com

Arkansas

Arkansas Paranormal Investigations

http://www.paranormalbeliever.com/

Centerton, Arkansas

See website for address and phone contact info

Spirit Seekers

http://www.thespiritseekers.org/

spirit@thespiritseekers.org

NWA Ghost Connection

http://www.ghostconnection.net/

NWAGHOSTCONNECTION@YAHOO.CO
M

Paranormal Studies of Arkansas

http://www.hauntedarkansas.net/Para
normalStudies/Paranormal.html

Contact form on website

ARPAST

![Arkansas Paranormal & Anomalous Studies Team banner]

ARPAST LLC
1818 N. Taylor, #337
Little Rock, AR. 72207

California

Bay Area Paranormal Investigations

http://www.bayareaparanormal.com/t
eam.html Paranormal investigation

contact@bayareaparanormal.com

Southern California Ghost Hunters
Society

http://www.scghs.com/

Please use online contact form

SpiritWorldOne Investigations

http://www.spirit-world-one-
investigations.com/

angie@spirit-world-one-
investigations.com

Pacific Paranormal

http://www.pacificparanormal.org/

P.O. Box 853
Bonita, CA 91908
dwalters@pacificparanormal.org

PhenomQuest Paranormal
Investigators - Los Angeles area

http://www.phenomquest.net/prodsite
/

7900 Nelson Rd.
Panorama City CA 91402

<u>Haunted and Paranormal Investigatons
of Northern California</u>

http://www.hpiparanormal.net/default.
asp

ghost@snmproductionsco.com

A famous picture taken with infrared
camera at a Toys R Us in Sunnyvale,
CA.

The man leaning against the window
was not seen by anyone present that
day, or on regular film used at the
same time.

Colorado

Western Colorado Paranormal
Research

http://westcoparanormal.com/

westco@westcoparanormal.com

Rocky Mountain Paranormal Research
Society

http://www.rockymountainparanormal
.com/

See website for contact information

ParaFPI (Littleton)

http://www.parafpi.com/

See website for info

Connecticut

Connecticut Paranormal Research Society

http://www.cprs.info/

See website for info

PROOF Paranormal-Connecticut

http://www.proofparanormal.com/proofct.html

proofct@proofparanormal.com

Northwest Connecticut Paranormal Society

http://www.northwestconnecticutparanormal.com/

nwcparanormal@sbcglobal.net

Delaware

Delaware Ghost Hunters

http://www.delawareghosthunters.co
m/Delaware Ghost Hunters

See website for more information.

Florida

Daytona Beach Paranormal Research
Group, Inc.

http://www.dbprginc.org/

We met Doris "Dusty" Smith at
Ghostock 4 February 1-4, 2007. She
was a dynamic, open, honest speaker
while describing her adventures during
a most atypical investigation, shown
on Discovery Channel as "A Haunting
in Florida, and detailed in her book,
**Dread and the Dead Filled the
Dunnam House.** My husband and I
finished most of the book on the way
home, and it was excellent as I
expected. Dusty seems to be very

thorough, professional, and dedicated to her work. We recommend her group, her tour (see Florida Ghost tours) and her book. See the website for contact information.

Secret Society of Paranormal Research (The Paranormal Stew)

http://destinshuttle.sslpowered.com/2/Stew.html

SCARDSPOOKY@YAHOO.COM

Paranormal Awareness Society

http://www.freewebs.com/paranormalawarenesssociety/

See website for more information

Southern Ghosts

http://www.southernghosts.com/cart/

info@southernghosts.com

Haunted Hunters PSI

http://www.hauntedhunterspsi.com/

Research@hauntedhuntersPSI.com

Georgia

West Georgia Paranormal Research
Society

http://www.wgprs.com/

WGPRS Investigations
c/o Joey Ward
144 Huel Road
Woodbury, Georgia 30293

Northwest Georgia Paranormal
Investigation Team

http://www.nwgapit.com/

This is also the home of Georgia
Paranormal Radio

mike@nwgpit.com

Georgia Ghost Society

http://www.georgiaghostsociety.com/i
ndex1.html

Visit the website for more info

Ghost Hounds

GHOST HOUNDS

Photo: Patrick Burns of Ghost Hounds

http://www.ghosthounds.com/

I am a member of Ghost Hounds and recently had the great experience of attending Ghoststock 4, the 4th of semi-annual paranormal conventions Patrick and his wife Pam host in Savannah, GA. I strongly recommend Ghost Hounds to anyone interested in paranormal investigation, either those dealing with a paranormal situation or those wanting to become investigators themselves, or just anyone with an interest or curiosity about ghosts. You can also see Patrick on Court TV's Haunting Evidence.

Media Inquiries-<u>678-524-7537</u>

All other inquiries:
<u>info@ghosthounds.com</u>

<u>Southern Ghost Hunters</u>

http://www.southernghosthunters.com
/

contact@southernghosthunters.com

<u>East Georgia Paranormal</u>

http://www.bobbysuniverse.net/

Eastgeorgiaparanormal2@yahoo.com

Hawaii

None so far

Idaho

<u>Idaho Paranormal Society</u>

http://www.idahoparanormal.com/pag
es/1/index.htm

help@idahoparanormal.com

Idaho Spirit Seekers

http://www.idahospiritseekers.com/

PO BOX 156
NAMPA IDAHO 83686
admin@idspiritskrs.co

Illinois

Crawford County Illinois Ghost Hunters
Society

http://www.crawfordcountyghosthunte
rs.com/

illinoishauntings@yahoo.com

Find more info on the website

Northern Illinois Paranormal Investigation Society

http://www.nipis.org/

SPLAT75@NIPIS.ORG

Springfield Ghost Society

http://www.springfieldghostsociety.com/

Springfield Ghost society also offers a free newsletter.

Springfield Ghost Society
200 State St
Rochester IL 62563

Haunted Chicago Paranormal Research and Investigation

http://www.hauntedchicago.com/

See website for info

Indiana

Indiana Paranormal Investigations

http://www.indianaparanormal.com/

maggie3@indy.rr.com

The DVD they offer of Central State is very interesting.

Central State, Historic Photograph

Indiana Ghost Trackers

http://www.lafayetteghosts.org/

igtlafayette@yahoo.com

Southern Indiana Paranormal Investigators

http://millersspooks.blogspot.com/

Very interesting blog spot, lots of videos

Johnson County Paranormal investigators

http://www.jcparanormal.com/

JCPI_Ghosthunter@yahoo.com

IOWA

Iowa Center for Paranormal Research

http://www.iowacenterforparanormalr esearch.com/

harleyd75@hotmail.com

rachbrian@hotmail.com

P.R.I.S.M.

http://www.doyouseedeadpeople.org/ video.html

Lots of videos and press coverage

Contact forms on website

Kansas

Kansas Paranormal Research and Investigation Site

http://www.kprishaunts.com/

See site for more info

Double A Paranormal Investigations

http://paragirl77.tripod.com/doubleaparaormal/

Kentucky

Ghost Chasers International

Ghost Hunter Shop
835 Porter Place
Lexington, KY 40508

Home of Patti Star and Chip Coffey
and their team

Kentucky Paranormal Investigations

http://kypinvestigations.tripod.com/

Phillip Brummett Jr.
P.O. Box 11725
Lexington, Ky. 40577

Dean Stephens
dean.stephens@insightbb.com

S.I.G.H.T.

http://www.sightonline.com/index.htm
l

8281 Dorinda Drive
Louisville, Kentucky 40258

Kentucky Shadow Chasers

http://kentuckyshadowchasers.com/

fleshia@kentuckyshadowchasers.com

Louisiana Paranormal Studies

http:/www.louisianaparanormalstudies
.com

See website for contact information

The Myrtles Plantation, historic picture

Louisiana Spirits

http://www.laspirits.com/

See website for info

New Orleans Paranormal Investigations

http://www.freewebs.com/lsh1/

ParaScienceTeam1@aol.com

Maine

Maine Supernatural Paranormal
Investigations

http://mysite.verizon.net/vzeqnk8x/pa
rainvestigate.html

eforester@verizon.net

Central Maine Researchers and
Investigators of the Paranormal

http://centralmaineparanormal.com/

centralmainerip@yahoo.com

Maryland

The Baltimore Society for Paranormal
Research

http://bsprnet.com/

E-mail vince@ghosttech.net

(410) 558-6224 for local callers in the
Baltimore, Maryland area and leave a
message
Or for those out of the calling area:
Call 1-800-699-2466 and key in the
mailbox code GHOSTS-1000 (or
446787-1000)

Maryland Paranormal Investigators

http://www.angelfire.com/md/MPInves
tigators/

snickrdos@angelfire.com

Massachussetts

New England Paranormal
investigations

http://www.newenglandparanormal.co
m/home.php

See website for more info

The New England Ghost Project

http://www.neghostproject.nstemp.co
m/index.html

1166 Merrimack Avenue

Dracut MA 01826

Other contact info on site

PROOF Massachussetts

http://proofparanormal.com/proofmas
s.html

proofmass@proofparanormal.com

Michigan

Grimstone Inc.

http://www.grimstone-
inc.com/main.html

See website for contact form and info

The Dead Watch Society

http://www.deadwatchsociety.com/

todd@deadwatchsociety.com

Shadow Land investigators

See the website for more information

Minnesota

Minnesota Paranormal Investigators

http://minnesotaparanormalinvestigators.com/

mnpig@netzero.com

Midnite Walkers Paranormal Research Society

http://midnite-walkers.com/

Contact form on website

Minnesota Ghost Hunters Society

http://www.mnghsc.com/

mnghsc@hotmail.com

Mississippi

Haunted Mississippi Paranormal
Research

http://www.hauntedmississippi.com/

Shadowz Paranormal

http://shadowzparanormal.com/

Shadowzhunters@aol.com

Missouri

Missouri Paranormal Research Society

http://www.missouriparanormal.com/

mike@missouriparanormal.com

Millers Paranormal Research

http://www.millersparanormalresearch
.com/

MPRBrenda@aol.com

Ghost Vigil Investigations

http://ghostvigil.com/modules/Home/

Contact forms on site

Ghosts & Haunts in Missouri

http://www.missourighosts.net/

Features a great list of haunted places
in Missouri

ghostvideo@missourighosts.net

Montana

Umbria Paranormal Research Group

http://www.angelfire.com/mt/morphe
us13/

morpheus0013@yahoo.com

Nebraska

PRISM

http://doyouseedeadpeople.org/inv_mystey_manor.html

Contact forms on the website

Great Plains Paranormal Research Society

http://www.gpprs.org/

Offers a free tutorial on EVPs

See website for more info

Nevada

Las Vegas Paranormal Investigations

http://www.lasvegasghosts.com/

lvparanormal@yahoo.com

lvpi.investigations@yahoo.com.

Las Vegas Society of Supernatural Investigation

http://lvssi.org/members1.htm

tina.carlson@lvssi.com

More contact info on website

Nevada Spirit Seekers

http://www.nvspiritseekers.com/conta
ct_us.html

WeHearDeadPeople@aol.com

New Hampshire

New Hampshire Paranormal

http://www.newhampshireparanormal.
com/

Register on the website

Ghost Quest

http://www.ravenduclos.com/homepa
ge.html

See website for contact info

New Jersey

Moorestown Ghost Research

http://www.moorestownghostresearch
.com/

Contact forms on website

New Jersey Ghost Hunters Society

http://www.njghs.net/

Offers "The Deadline" podcast

Ghost Hunters
PO Box 8018,
Parsippany, NJ 07054

New Jersey Ghost Organization

http://hometown.aol.com/strawberrifie
ld/index.html

strawberrifield@aol.com

North Jersey Paranormal Research

http://nnjpr.org/

MarkJ@nnjpr.org

New Mexico

Southwest Ghost Hunters Association

http://www.sgha.net/

ghost@sgha.net

Offers "The Graveyard Shift" radio program

New York

Paranormal Investigation of New York City

http://www.paranormal-nyc.com/

Dom@paranormal-nyc.com or

Dan S. @ Dan@paranormal-nyc.com

New York Ghost Chapter

http://www.newyorkghostchapter.com/

New YorkGC@aol.com

Western New York Paranormal

http://www.wnyparanormal.org/e107/news.php

Offers "The Other Side" radio

wnyparanormal@aol.com

Center for Paranormal Investigation

http://www.centerforparanormal.blogspot.com/

Director@weirdny.org
Director@centerforparanormal.org

North Carolina

Haunted North Carolina

http://www.hauntednc.com/

Haunted North Carolina, Inc.
P.O. Box 2192
Cary, NC 27512-2192
1-866-HAUNTNC (428-6862)

North Carolina Paranormal

http://www.ncparanormal.com/

julie@ncparanormal.com

Eastern Paranormal

http://www.easternparanormal.com/

gabreael@easternparanormal.com

L.E.M.U.R.

http://shadowboxent.brinkster.net/lem urhome.html

See website for more information

Regional Investigators of the Paranormal

http://ripgroup.com/

info@ripgroup.com

Also investigating in Kentucky, South Carolina and Virginia

North Dakota

NDSS

http://www.freewebs.com/ndspiritseekers/

See website for contact info

North Dakota Ghost Hunters and Paranormal investigators

http://ghostinvestigator.tripod.com/ndgis/

See website for more info

OHIO

Ohio Paranormal Investigation Network

http://www.angelfire.com/oh3/opin/

Ohio Paranormal Investigation Network
O.P.I.N.   Your mind.....

See contact form on website.

Ghost Hunters Ohio Search Team

http://www.ohioghosthunter.com/

look4ghst@aol.com

Southern Ohio Paranormal Research

http://www.southernohioparanormal.org/

See contact form on website

Ohio Ghost Researchers

http://www.ohio-ghost-researchers.com/

Ohio Ghost Researchers
106 W 58th St
ASHTABULA, OHIO 44004

The Ohio Paranormal Association

http://www.ghosttocoast.us/ghosthunterndtn.htm

See contact form on site

R.I.P. Ohio

vanishlkmagic102@neo.rr.com

SpiritFinders

ruth@spiritfinders.com

Ghost Corp

mail@ghostcorp.com

Oklahoma

Paranormal Investigation Team of Tulsa

http://www.pittok.com/home.html

P.I.T.T.
P.O. Box 803
Broken Arrow, OK 74013

<u>O.K.P.R.I.</u>

http://www.okpri.com/

okpri@okpri.com

<u>Southwest Oklahoma Ghost Chasers</u>

http://www.swogc.net/

See website for more information

<u>EERIE Oklahoma Paranormal Research</u>

http://www.eerieok.com/home.htm

tammy@eerieok.com

The former Tulsa Hex House, now an

allegedly haunted parking lot.

Oregon

Southern Oregon Paranormal Research
Group

http://www.soprg.org/

Contact form on website

Trail's End Paranormal Society

http://trailsendparanormalsociety.org/

PO Box 498
Oregon City, OR 97045-0027

trailsendparanormal@earthlink.net

Salem Paranormal

http://www.salemparanormal.com/ho
me.html

mike@salemparanormal.com

Pennsylvania

Pennsylvania State University
Paranormal Research Society

http://www.clubs.psu.edu/up/paranor
mal/

Paranormal Research Society
c/o Penn State University
125 HUB/ROBESON Center
University Park, PA 16802

NW PA Hauntings

http://www.nwpah.com/

lnwpah@zoominternet.net

Strange Happenings Ghost and Hauntings

http://www.strangehappenings.org/Pe
nnsylvania-Ghost-Hunters-Paranormal-
Investigators-In-Pennsylvania.htm

Offers free newsletter

ghosthunters@strangehappenings.org

Ghost Research Foundation

http://www.ghostsrus.com/

pineycreekpress@yahoo.com

Philadelphia Ghost Hunters Alliance

http://members.aol.com/Rayd8em/ind
ex.html

info@phillyghost.com

PHILADELPHIA GHOST HUNTERS ALLIANCE

Greater Pittsburgh Paranormal Society

http://members.aol.com/Rayd8em/index.html

See the website for information

Rhode Island

T.A.P.S.

http://the-atlantic-paranormal-society.com/

3208 Post Rd.

Warwick, RI 02886

Through T.A.P.S., personal appearances, the Sci Fi hit Ghost Hunters, T.A.P.S. Paramagazine, and now, Beyond Reality Radio and TAPS

Family Radio, Jason and Grant and
their team have probably done more
to promote the scientific approach
than any other currently active
organization,and have helped to set
the standards for non-profit
paranormal investigation.

Paranormal Investigators of Rhode
Island

http://paranormal31.tripod.com/invest
igators/

paranormal_investigators_RI@yahoo.c
om

The Rhode Island Paranormal
Research Group

http://www.triprg.com/index1.htm

triprg@yahoo.com

South Carolina

Low Country Paranormal
Investigations

http://www.triprg.com/index1.htm

Seeking_Spirits@hotmail.com

SC Ghosthunters

http://www.scghosthunters.com/

webmaster@scghosthunters.com

Paranormal Search and Investigation
Group

http://www.angelfire.com/ct2/PDIG/P
SIG1.html

Aurora_X@webtv.net

A picture from St. Phillips Cemetary,
Charleston, S.C., taken in the 80's.
Possibly the ghost of Sue Howard.

Upstate Ghost Hunters

http://www.upstateghosthunters.com/i
ndex.html

admin@upstateghosthunters.com

South Dakota

South Dakota Ghost Hunters

http://www.geocities.com/sdghosthunters/

sdghosthunters@yahoo.com

Tennessee

Tennessee Ghost Hunters

http://www.tnghosthunters.com/

Contact form on site

East Tennessee Paranormal Research Society

http://www.tnseeparanormal.com/

help@etprs.com

Memphis-MidSouth Ghost Hunters

http://www.memphisghosthunters.com/

P.O. Box 281254
Memphis, TN 38168

contact@memphisghosthunters.com

Tennessee Paranormal

http://tnparanormal.com/

See website for info

West Tennessee Ghost Hunters

http://groups.msn.com/WestTennesseeGhostHunters

See website for info

Middle Tennessee Paranormal
Research Group

http://www.hauntedsouls.com/MTPRS.html

(Haunted Souls)

Extensive forums

Cryptkeepers@hauntedsoul

Texas

Pararnormal Investigations of Texas

http://www.paratexas.com/

EVPgatekeeper@aol.com

Lone Star Spirits

http://www.lonestarspirits.org/

P.O. Box 683101
Houston, TX 77268-3101

info@lonestarspirits.org

PRTS

http://www.paranormaltexas.net/investigations.html

prts@paranormaltexas.net

Texas Ghost Hunters

http://www.texasghosthunters.com/

tgh@texasghosthunters.com

Corpus Christi Spook Central

http://ccspookcentral.com/

lil_angel@ccspookcentral.com

Ghost Seekers of Texas

http://www.ghostseekersoftexas.com/

info@ghostseekersoftexas.com

Utah

Paranormal Research of Utah

http://www.ghosthuntutah.com/

mike@ghosthuntutah.com

Utah Ghost Research and Investigation

See contact info on site

The Paranormal Investigations Team of Utah

http://www.piteamofutah.com/INVESTIGATIONS.html

michael@piteamofutah.com

Paranormal Utah

http://www.paranormalutah.com/

http://www.ugri.org/

Contact form on site

Vermont

V.A.P.O.R.

http://www.teamvapor.org/

teamvapor@msn.com

Virginia

Virginia Scientific Research Association

http://www.vsra.net/

keeler@vsra.net

CPRI

http://www.virginiaghosts.com/

info@virginiaghosts.com

Washington State

Washington State Paranormal investigations and Research

http://www.wspir.com/

darren@wspir.com

A.P.A.R.T. of Washington

http://www.apartofwa.com/

info@apartofwa.com

Southwest Washington Paranormal Research

http://www.swpr.org/

See website for info

Washington Historic Photo

A.G.H.O.S.T

http://www.aghost.us/

AGHOST@aghost.us

Washington D.C.

Washington D.C. Metro Area Ghost Watchers

http://www.dchauntings.com/

chief@dchauntings.com

West Virginia

<u>Mountaineer Ghosts Paranormal investigators</u>

http://mysite.verizon.net/vze836l6/index.html

GHosTsiTTeR@msn.com

<u>West Virginia Ghost Hunters</u>

http://ghosthunterwv.tripod.com/

DJCRUISE30@aol.com

Wisconsin

<u>Southern Wisconsin Paranormal Research Group</u>

http://www.paranormalresearchgroup.homestead.com/

ParanormalResearchGroup@yahoo.com

WIX

http://www.hauntedwi.com/

kchiv898@uwsp.edu

132 Knutzen Hall
Stevens Point, WI 54481

The Paranormal Investigations of Kenosha

http://www.kenoshaparanormal.com/

hardrockspiritchaser@yahoo.com

Chippewa Valley Paranormal Investigators

http://www.chippewavpi.com/

CVPI
PO Box 462
Chippewa Falls, WI 54729
admin@chippewavpi.com

Wyoming

Wyoming Paranormal

http://www.wyomingparanormal.com/

webmaster@wyomingpa

Real Ghosts, Ghost Hunting, and Quantum Physics
By Robin Renee Bridges

One of the benefits of a lifetime of afterlife communication is that I know a lot about ghosts ... what they are and what they're not. For instance, they're not "caught between worlds." And they don't need us to help them "move on." They're exactly where they're supposed to be. You don't honestly think that God, the Creator of the Universe, would leave their eternal fate in your and my hands, do you?

You CAN say that they are "earthbound," but that's because their consciousness never left the earth. And when you die, yours won't either. We're all right here together forever. That's just the nature of the afterlife. Yes, knowing the laws of the afterlife can make these things a lot clearer.

Lately, I've been researching what folks believe about ghosts and hauntings. I've investigated the investigations. Repeatedly I've read, "We don't use ouija boards, séances, mediums or occult methods." Yet it's common for ghost researchers to accept, as an underlying condition of their investigations, the erroneous claims of psychics, mediums, and channels.

I'm referring to such concepts as "caught between worlds," "unfinished business," "earthbound souls," and ghost children in distress. At the same time ominous warnings urge vigilant caution in case non-human demons and malevolent entities are encountered. Oh, and don't forget the Hollywood expression, "Go to the light." Scientific research can't be conducted properly on a foundation of superstition.

Let me tell you some things that are true about ghosts. Actually there are only two kinds of ghosts: real and not-real.

The real ghosts are everywhere. They're in your home, in your car, in your school, and in your dreams. Ghost researchers call these interactive ghosts. I call them soul-ghosts, or disincarnate souls. I don't care for the term, disembodied because they do have a body. We just can't see it for the same reason that we can't see sound waves and ultraviolet light. They're outside the range of our sentient boundary.

Soul-ghosts are interactive. They
reach out to you, and you feel no fear
... absolutely none. They envelop you
in a blanket of warm fuzzies. Real
ghosts can be mistaken for angels.
This isn't a paranormal experience. It's
a supernatural and spiritual
experience.

The not-real ghosts seem to be
everywhere too, but only for people
that believe they exist, or at least
believe that they might exist. They
rarely bother unbelievers. Ghost
researchers call the not-real ghosts ...
residual ghosts. These ghosts seem to
defy the Law of Conservation of Matter
and Energy because they pop in and
out of existence like virtual particles.
The appearance of this type of ghost
can be explained by quantum physics.
From the Copenhagen Interpretation,
which states that nothing is real until
you look at it, to the holographic
theory of the universe, all ghosts abide
by the laws of quantum physics.

People that experience residual ghosts
say that they seem to be caught in a
time-loop replaying the same scene
over and over. The above mentioned
physics also apply to residual ghosts
but with the addition of Schrodinger's
equations. For every "now" that we

experience, a positive wave flows into the future and a negative wave flows into the past like concentric ripples created by a rock thrown into a pond.

The fact that some people experience residual ghosts is due to normal functions of human consciousness. Although some might rather think of it as a "glitch." Residual ghosts are unusual and fascinating experiences with natural causes.

Briefly, a few more types of not-real ghosts are poltergeists, demons, and shadow people. Abnormal psychology applies to poltergeists and demons. The physiology of the eye accounts for shadow people.

So, what's the truth about ghosts? Do they exist? Yes, of course they do. Can the scientific method be used to investigate them? Yes, they use measurable amounts of energy. Can you record their voices and photograph ghosts? Yes, but one needs to be alert to pattern recognition tendencies.

The science of ghost investigation has the potential to make a huge difference in a society still tormented by superstition and fear. You have the equipment. You have the rationale. And you have the compassionate desire to help others.

Robbin Renee Bridges, a chaplain and grief counselor for more than thirty years, is the author of numerous published articles and the landmark book, "A Bridge of Love between Heaven and Earth: Self-Induced Contact in the Afterlife." For more articles about death, ghosts, and the nature of the souls in the afterlife visit http://www.spirit-sanctuary.org

Article Source: http://EzineArticles.com/?expert=Robin_Renee_Bridges

Haunted Hotels

"The dead

Say nothing

And the dead

Know much

And the dead

Hold under their tongues

A locked-up

Story."

-Carl Sandburg

Alabama

Hampton Inn Tutwiler

2021 Park Place
North, Birmingham, Alabama, USA 352
03
Tel: +1-205-322-2100 Fax: +1-205-325-1183

 Said to be haunted by the former owner, Colonel Tutwiler

Alaska

Golden North Hotel

3rd and Broadway St , Skagway, AK
(907) 983-2451

2 haunted rooms: 14 has a strange moving light and 23 has a ghost known as "Mary"

Arizona

The Gadsden Hotel

1046 G Avenue, Douglas, AZ (520) 364-4481

Has a history of its ghost on its website

Hotel San Carlos

202 N Central Ave, Phoenix, AZ (602) 253-4121

Mentions its female ghost in its history

Arkansas

Crescent Hotel

75 Prospect Ave , Eureka Springs, AR (501) 253-9766

Has a lot of information about its ghosts on its website, including a link to an article about the

"Ghost Hunters" episode featuring the Crescent.

California

Hotel del Coronado

500 Orange Ave, Coronado, CA (619) 435-6611

Mentions the ghost of Kate Morgan in its hotel history section

The Groveland Hotel

18767 Main St, Groveland, CA (209) 962-4000

Tells the story of "Lyle," the ghost of a former miner, on the website

The Queen Mary

1126 Queens Hwy, Long Beach, CA (310) 435-3511

Yes, the Queen Mary is a hotel, and famously haunted

Mendocino Hotel

45080 Main St, Mendocino, CA (707) 937-0511

Has link to ghost story article on website

Colorado

The Stanley Hotel

333 Wonderview, Estes Park, CO (970) 586-3371

Its real ghosts were the inspiration for Stephen King's "The Shining"

Connecticut

Homespun Farm

306 Preston Road, Griswold, CT (860) 376-5178

Has link to ghost article in newspaper on website

Florida

<u>Casablanca Inn</u>

24 Avenida Menendez, St. Augustine,
FL (904) 829-0928

Has story of "the lady with the lantern"
on the website

Georgia

<u>Jekyll Island Club Hotel</u>

371 Riverview Dr, Jekyll Island, GA
(912) 635-2600

The ghost will read your newspaper
and drink your coffee, they say

<u>17 Hundred 90</u>

307 E. President St, Savannah, GA
(912) 236-7122

Has a link to the ghost story

Hawaii

Hawaii has one that appears to be
very haunted, but they don't mention
their ghost,

so I don't feel comfortable listing them.

Idaho

Idanha Hotel

928 West Main Street
Boise, ID 83702

This hotel does not appear to have a website, but its ghost is mentioned in an article

from the Boise weekly, October, 2005, so I am assuming they do not mind being listed.

Illinois

Congress Plaza Hotel

520 South Michigan Avenue
Chicago, IL 60605
phone: 1-312-427-3800
fax: 312-427-2919

This hotel does not mention its ghost on its website, but it is mentioned numerous times on the Internet.

Indiana

The Story Inn

6404 South State Road
Nashville, IN
(800) 881-1183

The Story Inn mentions its Blue Lady
in its history and also has a link to a
special section about her.

Kansas

Kansas does not appear to have any
hotels that acknowledge their ghostly
visitors on their webpages

Kentucky

The Talbott Tavern

PO Box 365

107 West Stephen Foster

Bardstown, KY

(502) 348-3494

While the Talbott does not mention any haunted history directly, it does have links to several ghost hunting sites.

It is a very old former stagecoach inn, and was the site of a tragic fire in the 1990's.

The Seelbach Hilton

500 Fourth Avenue
Louisville, KY
(502) 585-3200

The Seelbach mentions its resident ghost in its history.

Louisiana

1891 Castle Inn

1539 4th Street
New Orleans, LA
(888) 826-0540

Only available for long stays, but proud of the ghosts and worth visiting

Hotel Monteleone

214 Royal Street
New Orleans, LA
(504) 523-3341

Has a whole section under "press" on hauntings

Myrtles Plantation

Myrtles Plantation Historic Picture

7747 U.S. Highway 61
St. Francisville, LA
(225) 635-6277

Yes, you can stay at one of the most haunted locations in America!

Massachussetts

Concord's Colonial Inn

48 Monument Square #3
Concord, MA
(978) 369-9200

Has a section about Room 24 under "About the Inn"

Lizzie Borden Bed & Breakfast

92 Second St
Fall River, MA
(508) 675-7333

I honestly don't know why anyone would want to stay here, but you can. Even the pictures of the rooms make me feel ill.

Michigan

The Holly Hotel

Sort of a cheat, since it's no longer a hotel, but a restaurant. Still, it's proud of its ghosts and worth a visit.

Minnesota

Thayer's Historic Bed & Breakfast

60 West Elm St
Annandale, MN
(800) 944-6595

Says it is haunted right on the home
page

Mississippi

Sadly, I cannot find a Mississippi hotel that
advertises its ghosts.

Missouri

Grand Avenue Bed & Breakfast

1615 Grand Ave
Carthage, MO
(417) 358-7265

Mentions its cigar-smoking ghost in its
history

Montana

So far, no hotels in Montana want to
brag about their ghosts.

Nevada

Only one famous hotel that is known to be haunted in Nevada so far, and it is in a ghost town and not open to the public: The Goldfield Hotel in Goldfield, NV. It is closed off! Get permission if you want to see inside!

New Jersey

The Flanders Hotel

719 11th St
Ocean City, NJ
(609) 399-1000

A link to the story of the happy ghost, Emily, is under the history section of the website.

New Mexico

The St. James Hotel

17th & Collinson
Cimarron, NM
(505) 376-2664

Mentions ghosts on the home page

The Lodge at Cloudcroft

1 Corona Place
Cloudcroft, NM
(505) 682-2566

Mentions ghostly inhabitants on the
home page

New York

The Hotel Chelsea

222 W. 23rd St
New York, NY 10011 [map]
Tel +1 212 243 3700
UK +44 (20) 8133 9533
Japan +81 (50) 5534 6659

The Hotel Chelsea does not actually
mention its ghosts per se, but I know
they would not mind. Dylan Thomas
stayed there, and lots of other highly
creative people.

North Carolina

While a number of hotels are listed in
several directories on the Internet,
none of them I can find are bragging
about it.

North Dakota

<u>Rough Riders Hotel</u>

PO Box 198
301 5th Street
Medora, ND 58645
medora@medora.com
1-800-633-6721
1-701-623-4444
1-701-623-4494 (fax)

While they do not mention ghosts, a
local ghost hunting group states that
the hotel is haunted by a child. They
do mention lore and legend, so would
probably be open to ghost enthusiasts.

Ohio

The Buxton Inn

313 E. Broadway
Granville, OH
(740) 587-0001

This inn claims to be "America's most ghostly country inn."

Oklahoma

The Stone Lion Inn

1016 West Warner
Guthrie, OK
(405) 282-0012

The title of the home page is "The Haunted Stone Lion Inn."

Oregon

There is a very famous haunted hotel in Oregon, but since they don't mention their ghost anywhere on their website, I don't want to mention them here.

Pennsylvania

<u>The Farnsworth House Inn</u>

401 Baltimore St
Gettysburg, PA
(717) 334-8838

In the History of the Inn section of the website, brags of being documented as the 7th most haunted Inn in America.

R&R Station Inn

19 West Main Street
Mt. Pleasant, PA 15666
724-547-7545

Has a link to the trailer for a film
made about its haunting.

New Hope's 1970 Wedgewood Inn

111 West Bridge St Main St
New Hope, PA
(215) 862-2570

Mentions having been featured in a
documentary about ghost stories on
the home page.

Rhode Island

I could not find a Rhode Island hotel
willing to brag about its ghosts.

South Carolina

Battery Carriage House Inn

20 S. Battery
Charleston, South Carolina (SC) 29401
Telephone: 843-727-3100
Fax: 843-727-3130
Toll Free: 1-800-775-5575

Has a link to "ghost sightings"

South Dakota

Bullock Hotel

633 Main Street
Historic Deadwood,
South Dakota 57732
(ph) 800-336-1876

As a huge fan of the television series,
"Deadwood," I am pleased to learn
that Seth Bullock still looks out for his

hotel, and his ghost gets a fond mention on the Bullock Hotel page.

Tennessee

To my great surprise, I cannot find any hotels mentioning their ghosts in very haunted Tennessee.

Texas

The Menger Hotel

204 Alamo Plaza
San Antonio, TX 78205
Tel: (210) 223-4361
Fax: (210) 228-0022
Email:
almapuente@1859historichotels.com

Has a link to Ghost Sightings on the home page

Utah

I was unable to find any hotels mentioning their ghosts in Utah.

Vermont

The Green Mountain Inn
18 Main Street
Stowe, Vermont 05672

800-253-7302
802-253-7301

Has a link to "The Legend of Boots
Betty"

Virginia

Virginia has a lot of haunted hotels.
This is a fact. But none of these hotels
mention their ghosts on their pages,
so I won't mention them here.

Washington

Thornewoode Castle

Tacoma, WA
(253) 584-4393

This fascinating place, where "Rose Red" was filmed, has a link to a page entitlted "Haunted Castle."

Washington DC

Washington DC knows how to keep a secret. None of the allegedly haunted hotels are mentioning their ghosts on their websites.

West Virginia

I found no hotels willing to talk about their ghosts in West Virginia.

Wisconsin

The Karsten Inn

Kewaunee, Wisconsin
920-388-3800
Toll Free 800-277-2132

Has a link to a newspaper article about
its ghosts

Wyoming

Buffalo Bill's Irma Hotel

1192 Sheridan Avenue
Cody, WY 82414
Tel: 307-587-4221
Fax: 307-587-1775
1-800-745-IRMA
Email: irmahotel@bresnan.net

This hotel, built by Buffalo Bill Cody,
does not mention its ghost, but it is
mentioned on the official Wyoming
tourism site, and that is good enough
for me.

A FINAL WORD:

Dear Reader,
I hope you enjoy this book as much as I have enjoyed writing it. If you know of tours, groups, or hotels I have missed, or if you have articles or poems you would like me to consider for the next edition, please email me at starmac@comcast.net. I especially would love to have your well-written reviews of ghost tours. Please also visit the original source for much of this material, my website, Ghost to Coast.us at http://www.ghosttocoast.us.

Blessed be,

Rhetta

Printed in the United States
90248LV00005B/174/A